IT'S TIME TO EAT CRENSHAW MELONS

It's Time to Eat CRENSHAW MELONS

Walter the Educator

Silent King Books
A WhichHead Entertainment Imprint

Copyright © 2024 by Walter the Educator

All rights reserved. No part of this book may be reproduced in any manner whatsoever without written per- mission except in the case of brief quotations embodied in critical articles and reviews.

First Printing, 2024

Disclaimer

This book is a literary work; the story is not about specific persons, locations, situations, and/or circumstances unless mentioned in a historical context. Any resemblance to real persons, locations, situations, and/or circumstances is coincidental. This book is for entertainment and informational purposes only. The author and publisher offer this information without warranties expressed or implied. No matter the grounds, neither the author nor the publisher will be accountable for any losses, injuries, or other damages caused by the reader's use of this book. The use of this book acknowledges an understanding and acceptance of this disclaimer.

It's Time to Eat CRENSHAW MELONS is a collectible early learning book by Walter the Educator suitable for all ages belonging to Walter the Educator's Time to Eat Book Series. Collect more books at WaltertheEducator.com

USE THE EXTRA SPACE TO TAKE NOTES AND DOCUMENT YOUR MEMORIES

CRENSHAW MELONS

It's time to eat a melon so sweet,

It's Time to Eat Crenshaw Melons

Crenshaw melons are such a treat!

Big and round, with a golden glow,

Their juicy goodness is sure to show.

Cut them open, what do you see?

Bright orange flesh, sweet as can be!

A fruity scent that fills the air,

It's time to share this treat so rare.

Scoop it out or slice it thin,

Take a bite, and let joy begin!

Soft and tender, bursting with taste,

Crenshaw melons are never a waste.

They grow in fields where the sun shines bright,

Soaking up warmth from morning to night.

Picked when ripe, they're ready to eat,

A summer snack that's hard to beat.

It's Time to Eat
Crenshaw Melons

Rich in vitamins, good for you,

Crenshaw melons help you, too!

They keep you strong and feeling great,

A healthy snack that's first-rate.

Blend them in smoothies, cool and nice,

Or enjoy them fresh, without any ice.

In fruit salads, they're the star,

A melon so sweet, it goes far!

At picnics, parties, or at the park,

Crenshaw melons bring a spark.

Bright and juicy, every bite,

Fills your tummy with pure delight.

Don't forget the seeds inside,

Save them for planting far and wide.

Grow more melons, big and round,

It's Time to Eat
Crenshaw Melons

In sunny fields or backyard ground.

When the sun is high, and you need to cool,

Crenshaw melons are the perfect rule.

Refresh your day, feel the fun,

With melons sweet for everyone.

So grab a melon, let's all eat,

A snack that's juicy, fresh, and sweet.

Crenshaw melons are simply divine,

It's Time to Eat
Crenshaw Melons

A tasty treasure, every time!

ABOUT THE CREATOR

Walter the Educator is one of the pseudonyms for Walter Anderson. Formally educated in Chemistry, Business, and Education, he is an educator, an author, a diverse entrepreneur, and he is the son of a disabled war veteran. "Walter the Educator" shares his time between educating and creating. He holds interests and owns several creative projects that entertain, enlighten, enhance, and educate, hoping to inspire and motivate you. Follow, find new works, and stay up to date with Walter the Educator™

at WaltertheEducator.com

www.ingramcontent.com/pod-product-compliance
Lightning Source LLC
LaVergne TN
LVHW052011060526
838201LV00059B/3977